HOW DOES IT WORK?

SMART HOMES

by Nikole Brooks Bethea

pogo

Ideas for Parents and Teachers

Pogo Books let children practice reading informational text while introducing them to nonfiction features such as headings, labels, sidebars, maps, and diagrams, as well as a table of contents, glossary, and index.

Carefully leveled text with a strong photo match offers early fluent readers the support they need to succeed.

Before Reading

- "Walk" through the book and point out the various nonfiction features. Ask the student what purpose each feature serves.
- Look at the glossary together. Read and discuss the words.

Read the Book

- Have the child read the book independently.
- Invite him or her to list questions that arise from reading.

After Reading

- Discuss the child's questions. Talk about how he or she might find answers to those questions.
- Prompt the child to think more. Ask: Have you ever used a smart device? What did it do? What made it "smart"?

Pogo Books are published by Jump!
5357 Penn Avenue South
Minneapolis, MN 55419
www.jumplibrary.com

Library of Congress Cataloging-in-Publication Data

Names: Bethea, Nikole Brooks, author.
Title: Smart homes / by Nikole Brooks Bethea.
Description: Minneapolis, MN: Jump!, [2021]
Series: How does it work?
Includes index. | Audience: Ages 7-10.
Identifiers: LCCN 2020028272 (print)
LCCN 2020028273 (ebook)
ISBN 9781645277835 (hardcover)
ISBN 9781645277842 (paperback)
ISBN 9781645277859 (ebook)
Subjects: LCSH: Home automation–Juvenile literature.
Classification: LCC TK7881.25 .B48 2021 (print)
LCC TK7881.25 (ebook) | DDC 643/.6–dc23
LC record available at https://lccn.loc.gov/2020028272
LC ebook record available at https://lccn.loc.gov/2020028273

Editor: Eliza Leahy
Designer: Molly Ballanger

Photo Credits: alice-photo/Shutterstock, cover (phone); Imagenet/Shutterstock, cover (house); MAHATHIR MOHD YASIN/Shutterstock, 1; Christian Horz/Shutterstock, 3; Shutterstock, 4, 6-7 (foreground), 8; LightField Studios/Shutterstock, 5 (foreground); Artazum/Shutterstock, 5 (background); Yuriy Maksymiv/Shutterstock, 6-7 (background); Vantage_DS/Shutterstock, 9; AnnaStills/Stock, 10-11; picturepixx/Shutterstock, 12-13 (foreground); aslysun/Shutterstock, 12-13 (background); Prostock-studio/Shutterstock, 14; canbedone/Shutterstock, 15 (foreground); tcharts/Shutterstock, 15 (background); Makeda Art/Shutterstock, 16; Evgeny Karandaev/Dreamstime, 16-17 (background); Pixel-Shot/Shutterstock, 16-17 (phone); Monkey Business Images/Shutterstock, 18-19; Noel Hendrickson/Getty, 20-21; Joni Hanebutt/Shutterstock, 23.

Printed in the United States of America at Corporate Graphics in North Mankato, Minnesota.

TABLE OF CONTENTS

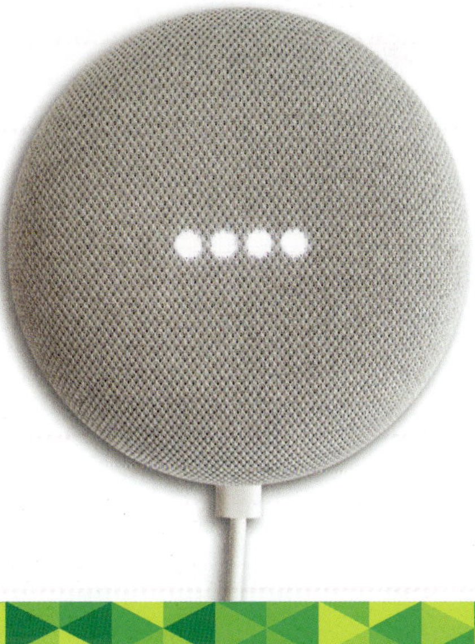

CHAPTER 1

WHAT ARE SMART HOMES?

Ding! You get a text. It is from the refrigerator. It says you are out of milk. It creates a shopping list.

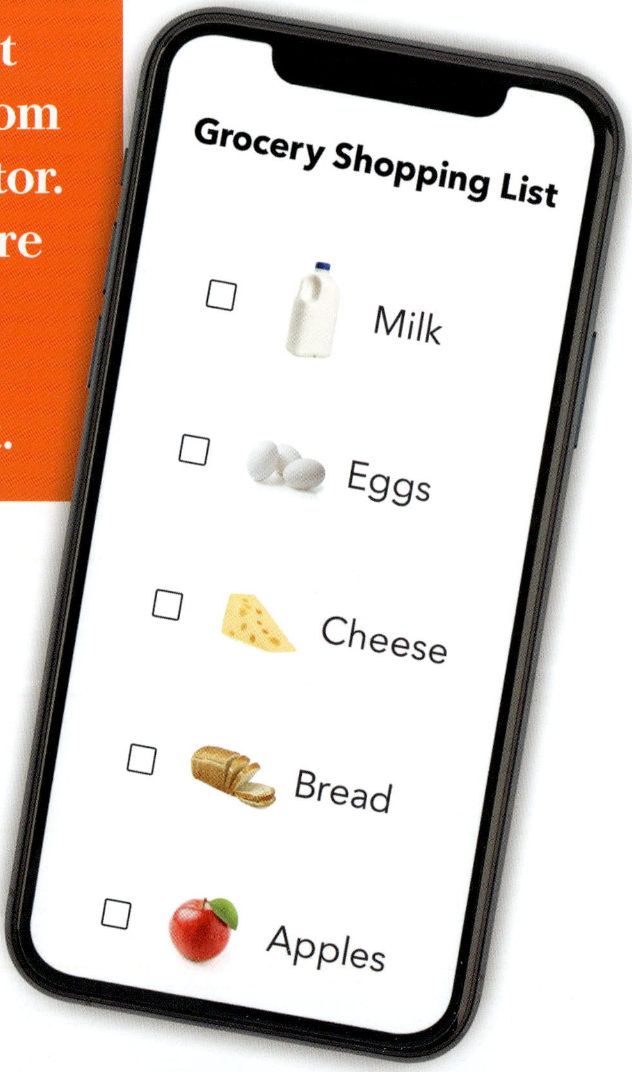

Then you walk into your home. You say, "Turn on the air conditioner." Cool air flows. You say, "Dim the lights." The lights dim. Can you do this? If you are in a **smart home**, you can!

A smart home uses **smart devices** and **appliances**. These connect to the internet. They exchange **data** with other smart devices. Apps on a smartphone or tablet control the devices. A home with many smart devices needs many apps to control them.

DID YOU KNOW?

Before **Wi-Fi**, there was another kind of smart home. It was called X10. It was created in the 1970s. Some homes still use it. Signals are sent to and from devices through electrical wiring.

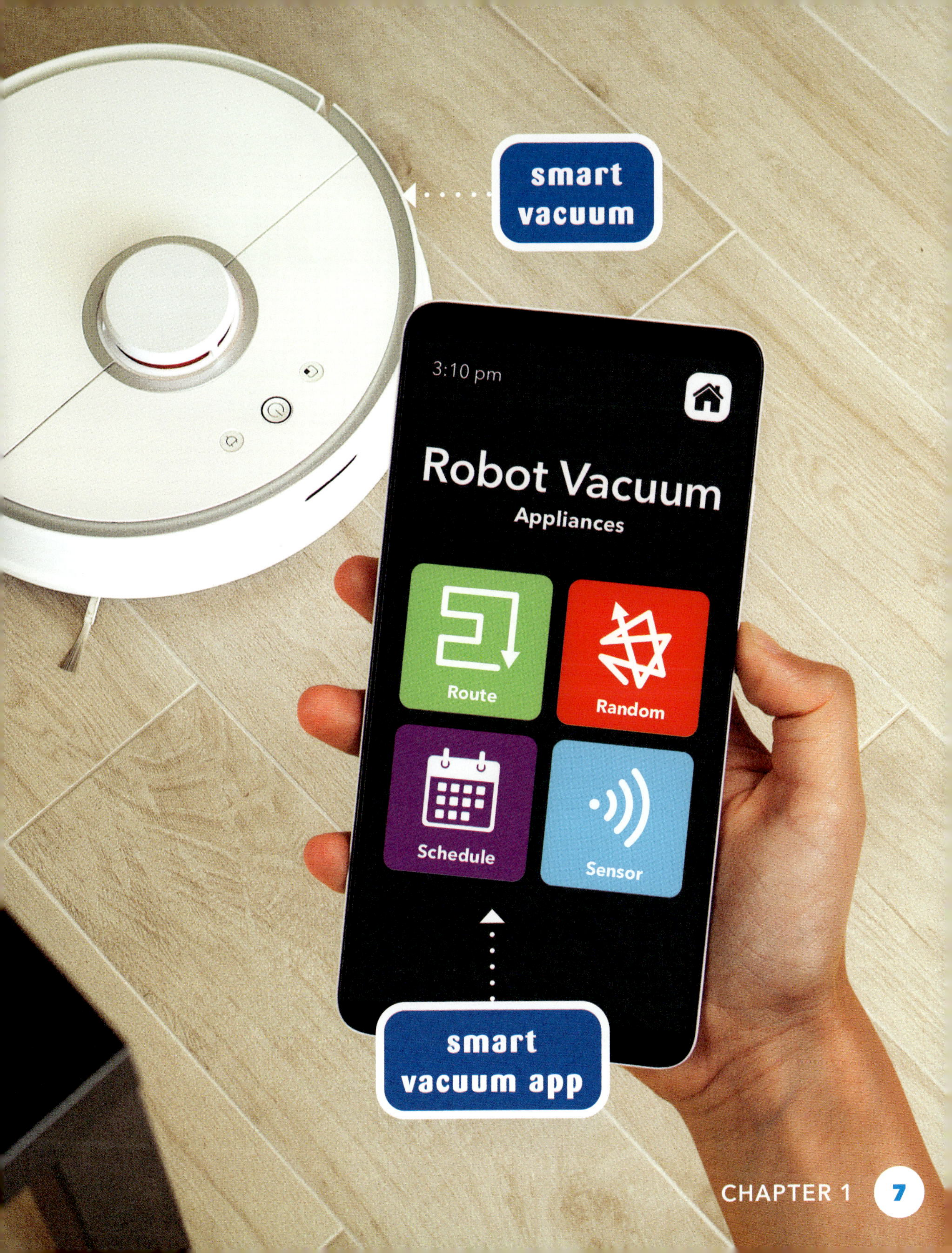
smart
vacuum
3:10 pm
Robot Vacuum
Appliances
Route
Random
Schedule
Sensor
smart
vacuum app

CHAPTER 2

SMART HOME HUBS

A **hub** allows all the devices to interact. It connects to smart devices through Wi-Fi, **Bluetooth**, smartphones, or **personal area networks**.

You give the hub a command. How? You open an app. Do you want to play music? You can control it through your hub's app.

The hub sends out **radio waves**. A device receives the signals. They tell the device what to do. One example is wireless headphones. In this case, the radio waves are turned into sound.

TAKE A LOOK!

A hub acts as the brain of a smart home. Take a look!

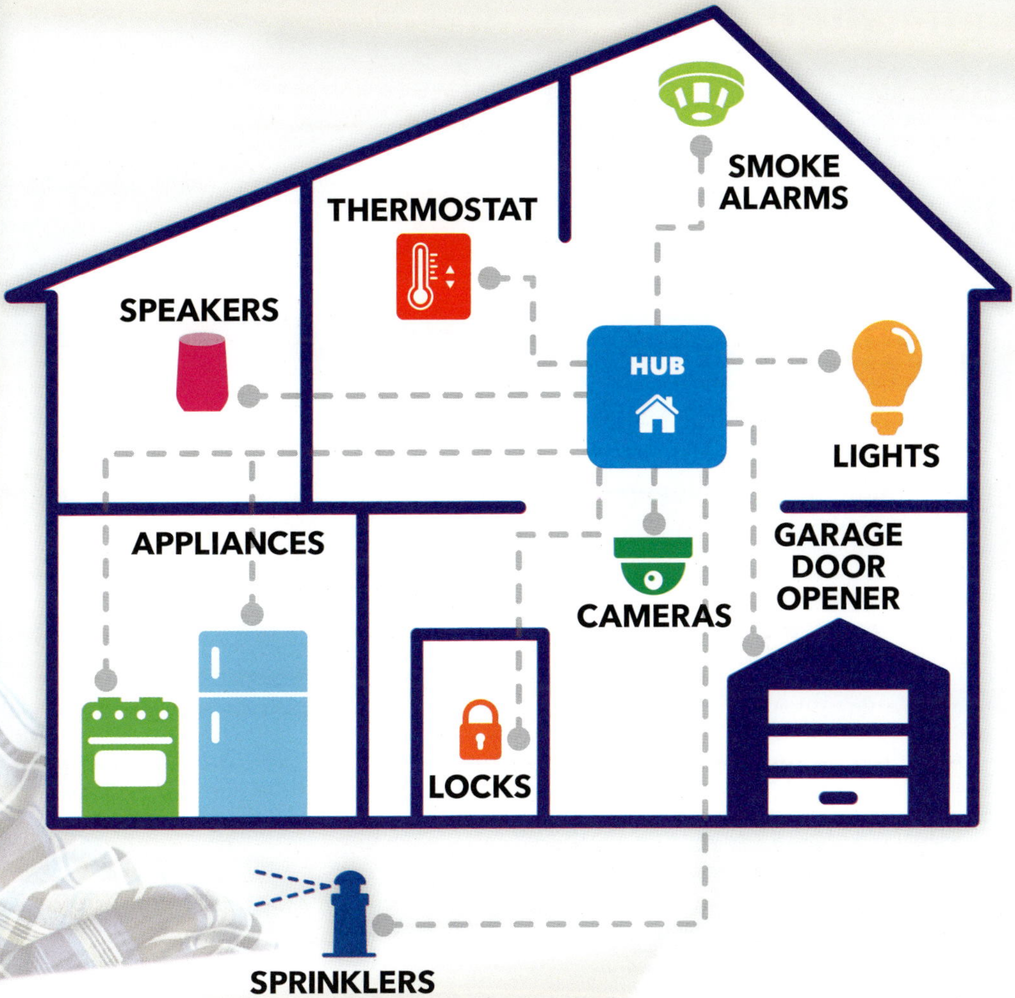

Some devices respond to voice commands. How? They are **programmed** to recognize a keyword. It may be the name of the device. You say the keyword. Then the device's microphone begins recording. It sends the recording over the internet to the device company's **server**. Speech is turned into text commands. The device performs the task.

DID YOU KNOW?

You can ask smart speakers to make a phone call. You can ask them for the weather forecast. Smart speakers can play music. They can set alarms, too.

smart
speaker

CHAPTER 3

SMART HOMES HELP

Smart homes are **efficient**. They save energy. Did you forget to turn the lights off before you left home? You can turn them off from your phone!

They can help save water, too. How? Smart sprinklers monitor weather. Is it raining? They will not water the lawn.

They also provide **security**. Did you hear the doorbell? Your phone can connect to a camera outside. You can check your phone to see who is there. Some systems even let you talk to the person at your door.

FRONT DOOR

55°
6:55 pm
NEWS
CHANNELS
SETTINGS
SMART TV
Streaming
Internet
Live TV
Movies

Smart homes are also **convenient**. Do you want to watch a movie? Smart TVs can play video from the internet. Are guests coming over? Use an app to start the vacuum. Did you forget to make a grocery list? Check the camera inside your refrigerator. You can see what you need to buy.

What will smart homes of the future do? Will they spot health problems? Will they have robots that can sense your feelings? What smart devices would you like in your future home?

DID YOU KNOW?

Bill Gates is a cofounder of Microsoft. Guests at his home wear a pin. It connects to a hub. It controls lighting and temperature as the guests move through the home.

ACTIVITIES & TOOLS

TRY THIS!

MAKE A SMART HOME PLAN

Think about which devices you would like in your ideal smart home. Then make a smart home plan!

What You Need:

- pencil
- paper
- ruler
- crayons, colored pencils, or markers

❶ Using the pencil, paper, and ruler, draw the floor plan of a home you might like to have one day.

❷ Think about what kinds of devices you will want. What devices will you have in the kitchen? What devices will you have for security and entertainment? Where will you place your smart home hub?

❸ Draw your dream smart devices where you want them.

❹ After you have completed your smart home plan, color it in.

GLOSSARY

appliances: Machines created to do certain jobs; toasters, washing machines, and hair dryers are appliances.

Bluetooth: Wireless technology that exchanges data over short distances.

convenient: Allowing you to do something without trouble.

data: Information that is produced by or stored in a computer.

efficient: Using less energy to perform a task.

hub: A central connection device that allows communication of multiple devices over a network.

personal area networks: Networks organized around a person and the devices nearby, such as a computer, printer, phone, and tablet.

programmed: Coded to perform a particular action.

radio waves: Forms of electromagnetic radiation that can be used in communications, such as radio, mobile phones, and television.

security: Protection from danger.

server: A computer, device, or program that provides data or manages resources for other computers.

smart devices: Electronic devices that are connected to other devices and the internet to exchange data.

smart home: A home in which appliances and devices can be remotely controlled with an internet connection.

Wi-Fi: A wireless technology that allows computers and devices to communicate.

INDEX

TO LEARN MORE

Finding more information is as easy as 1, 2, 3.

1. Go to www.factsurfer.com
2. Enter "smarthomes" into the search box.
3. Choose your book to see a list of websites.

FACT SURFER